CONTENTS

Hamlyn Essential

INDIAN

Hamlyn Essential
INDIAN

HAMLYN

First published in Great Britain in 1999 by Hamlyn
an imprint of Octopus Publishing Group Limited
2–4 Heron Quays, London E14 4JP

Designed and produced by SP Creative Design
Linden House, Kings Road, Bury St Edmunds, Suffolk, England
Editor and writer: Heather Thomas
Art director: Al Rockall
Designer: Rolando Ugolini

ISBN 0600 59635 4

A CIP catalogue record for this book is available from the
British Library

Produced by Toppan
Printed and bound in China

Acknowledgements
Special photography: James Murphy
Step-by-step photography: GGS Photographics, Norwich
Food preparation: Jane Stevenson and Caroline Stevens
Styling: Jane McLeish

Notes
1. Standard spoon measurements are used in all recipes.
1 tablespoon = one 15ml spoon
1 teaspoon = one 5ml spoon

2. Both imperial and metric measurements have been
given in all recipes. Use one set of measurements
only and not a mixture of both.

3. Eggs should be medium unless otherwise stated.

4. Milk should be full fat unless otherwise stated.

5. Fresh herbs should be used unless otherwise stated.
If unavailable, use dried herbs as an alternative, but halve
the quantities stated.

6. Ovens should be preheated to the specified temperature. If
using a fan assisted oven, follow the manufacturer's instructions
for adjusting the time and temperature.

INTRODUCTION

India is a large and diverse country with variations not only in climate and geography but also in culture, religion, customs and cooking. There are many regional cookery styles, culinary techniques and ingredients. For instance, barbecue-style tandoori food is the norm in northern India. The meat is marinated and then cooked over a charcoal fire in a *tandoor,* a beehive-shaped clay oven. In Delhi, presentation of food is very important and the dishes still reflect the style of those served to the Moghul emperors of the past. From central India come quickly-cooked vegetable dishes with a drier texture, whereas southern India is renowned for its fiery hot curries, often enhanced with coconut. The best seafood comes from Kerala and the southern coast where various *masalas* (spice mixtures) have evolved.

The dominant religion is Hinduism; most Hindus are vegetarian, although some eat meat, with the exception of beef. The Sikhs and Muslims eat meat, although the Muslims do not eat pork. However, what all Indians share is a love of spices, and these are the common denominator in Indian food. Of course, there are regional variations in the quantities and combinations of spices used in different dishes.

Indian cooks always try to produce a balanced meal consisting of several dishes which are served simultaneously. Usually there is a fish or meat dish, or both (or pulses if the family is vegetarian), served with vegetable dishes, bread or rice, a salad, yogurt and a selection of chutneys and relishes. Snack foods, such as samosas and pakoras, are eaten throughout the day rather than as part of a meal. In addition, there is an attempt to balance the colours, flavours and textures of the dishes, and thus really hot spicy dishes are balanced by cool, refreshing ones, and dry curries by moist ones.

A new exciting development in Indian food to arrive in Western countries is Balti cooking. These quickly-cooked medium or hot curries are made in the traditional *Karhai,* the Indian equivalent of a wok. It is a two-handled cast-iron pan with a rounded base for better, quicker heat distribution. Many of the dishes in this book are cooked in the Balti style.

Aniseed

These liquorice-flavoured seeds are often used in making chutneys and sweet confectionery. Aniseed may also be used in powdered form for flavouring meat and vegetable dishes.

Besan

This is yellow flour made from ground chick peas. It is always sifted thoroughly before use to remove any lumps that may form during storage. Another flour is gram flour, made from ground pulses.

Cardamoms

These may be large black seed pods or smaller green ones. The pods may be used whole to scent and flavour rice, meat and vegetable dishes, pilaus, biriyanis and sweets. The pods are always removed and discarded before serving. The seeds may also be ground and sprinkled over vegetable dishes.

Chillies

Red and green chillies may be used fresh or dried. There are many different varieties and these vary in their heat and intensity. You should always take care when handling chillies as the hot seeds can burn your skin. Avoid contact particularly with your face and eyes, and always wash your hands immediately afterwards. You can store unwashed whole chillies in a plastic bag in the refrigerator. If you do not like really hot curries, you can add the chilli flesh to the dish but omit the seeds.

Cinnamon

The dried bark quills of the cinnamon tree can be used whole or ground. They are used throughout India to flavour a wide range of sweet and savoury dishes. Cinnamon sticks are used whole to impart an aromatic flavour to many meat and rice dishes, in which case they are removed before serving and are not eaten.

Cloves

These are the dried flower buds of a plant in the myrtle family. They add a very distinctive spicy flavour to many classic recipes, and are used whole in curries and rice dishes, or ground in fruit desserts.

Coconut

Both the flesh and juice of the coconut are used to enhance many curries and desserts. When buying fresh coconuts, they should always feel heavy and full of juice when shaken gently. You can make a hole in the shell to drain out the liquid inside, and then break open the shell to prize out the flesh. To make coconut milk, the juice is mixed with the grated flesh, or you can blend desiccated coconut with boiling water, leave it to infuse and then strain it. Alternatively, you can buy ready-mixed coconut milk in cartons or cans in most supermarkets. It is also available in powdered form.

Coriander

The distinctive, delicately spicy flavour of fresh coriander makes it the Indians' favourite herb. The leaves are used as a garnish and for flavouring curries and chutneys, while the seeds may be added, whole or ground, to vegetable, pulse and grain dishes, and to garam masala.

Cumin

These seeds may be black or white and may be used whole or ground, especially in making garam masala and curry powders. The brownish coloured seeds which are usually bought whole or ground are white cumin. The seeds are often roasted before adding to dishes; this yields a marvellous aroma and slightly astringent flavour to the finished dish.

Fennel

These aniseed-flavoured seeds are often dry-roasted or flash-fried to make their flavour more intense. They can also be crushed and added to curries. Sometimes the seeds are chewed as an aid to digestion.

Fenugreek

Again, the seeds may be used whole or ground, but because of their slightly bitter flavour they should always be used sparingly. The seeds and leaves of the plant are often used to flavour vegetable curries.

Garam masala

Although you can buy this spicy mixture ready blended, it is always better to follow the example of Indian cooks and make your own. Garam masala is an aromatic mixture of ground spices, usually black peppercorns, cinnamon, cloves, coriander and cumin. They are dry-fried before grinding, and then used as a flavouring for a wide range of savoury dishes or as a garnish, sprinkled over meat, vegetables and cooked pulses.

Ghee

Clarified, unsalted butter, known as ghee, is often used as cooking fat, especially in southern India. The advantage of using ghee, as opposed to butter and most cooking oils, is that it can withstand higher temperatures without burning. You can buy it in cans or make it yourself.

Ginger

Sometimes called green ginger, fresh root ginger is actually a rhizome. It must be peeled before using and then it can be grated, crushed, sliced or chopped. Ginger blends easily with garlic, spring onions and chillies and adds a pungent flavour to many rice dishes, meat curries and desserts. It may also be bought dried, ground, crystallized or preserved in syrup.

Kalonji

These teardrop-shaped small black onion seeds are often added to vegetable curries, or they may be sprinkled on naan bread before baking.

Mango powder

This is made from dried unripe mango slices which are processed to a fine powder. It has a sour, rather sharp flavour and is often used as a substitute for tamarind pulp in curries.

Mustard seeds

You can buy black, brown or white varieties. Mustard seeds are often dry-roasted or flash-fried before using, usually in pulse and vegetable curries, to release their nutty flavour.

Palm sugar

This is sold in thin blocks and is known as *gula jawa* or *jula malaka*. If you cannot obtain it, you can substitute ordinary soft brown sugar in most recipes.

Poppy seeds

These may be used for thickening curries or to add a nutty flavour and crunchy texture to many Indian savoury dishes, breads and salads.

Pulses

There are over sixty varieties of pulses in India, including chick peas, black grams, red and yellow lentils, whole peas and pigeon peas. Pulses should always be rinsed in several changes of cold water before using and pre-soaked. Do not add salt during cooking as it can harden them; always season to taste afterwards.

Saffron

The world's most expensive spice, saffron is made from the orange stamens of crocuses. It takes literally thousands of crocuses to make just 25g/1oz of saffron! It can be bought ground or in threads and is used for colouring and flavouring rice dishes, biriyanis, sweets, cakes and puddings. If using saffron threads, soak them in hot water for 15 minutes before using. Add them to the dish with the soaking liquid.

Tamarind

The dried fruit of the tamarind tree is often known as 'Indian dates' because of its sticky appearance. The pods or pulp are soaked in hot water to make tamarind water, which adds an acidic sharpness to many dishes.

Turmeric

Fresh turmeric resembles root ginger, but it is usually sold and used in its ground form. The bright yellow powder gives a golden colour to many rice dishes and curries, but it should be used sparingly as the flavour can be overwhelming.

Varak

A popular edible garnish for many Indian festive dishes, both sweet and savoury. It is a form of thin silver leaf, which may be sold in sheets or broken up in jars. Never use aluminium foil as a substitute!

Utensils and equipment

Balti pan or karhai: this is a deep pan with rounded handles on opposite sides and a rounded base for more efficient heat distribution. It is used for cooking Balti-style dishes – curries which are cooked quickly. It is similar to a Chinese wok and originates from Pakistan.

Mortar and pestle: this can be used for grinding spices, although in many Indian regions a stone and slab are more common.

FISH AND COCONUT SOUP

Myhee molee shorva

500g/1lb monkfish or halibut fillet, skinned and cubed

salt

25g/1oz desiccated coconut

6 shallots

6 almonds, blanched

2 garlic cloves, peeled

2.5cm/1 inch piece root ginger, peeled and sliced

2 blades lemon grass, trimmed

2-3 teaspoons turmeric

3 tablespoons oil

1 quantity coconut milk (see page 110)

1 red chilli, seeded and sliced

1 quantity coconut cream (see page 110)

fresh coriander leaves, to garnish

1 Sprinkle the fish with salt. Place the coconut in a wok and heat gently until it is golden and crisp. Remove from the wok and pound until oily. Set aside.

2 Purée the shallots, almonds, garlic, ginger and 6cm/2½ inches from the root end of the lemon grass (reserving the remainder) in a blender or food processor. Add the turmeric.

3 Heat the oil in a wok or saucepan and fry the puréed mixture for a few minutes. Add the coconut milk and bring to the boil, stirring constantly. Stir in the fish, chilli and the remaining lemon grass. Cook over gentle heat for about 5 minutes.

4 Stir in the pounded coconut and cook for a further 5 minutes. Remove the blades of lemon grass and stir in the coconut cream. Serve hot, garnished with coriander.

PREPARATION: 25 MINUTES
COOKING: 15–20 MINUTES
SERVES: 4

SPICED CHICKEN SOUP

Murghi shorva

1 Put the water in a large saucepan and bring to the boil. Add the chicken and prawns with a little seasoning, then cover and simmer gently for 40 minutes. Strain, reserving 1.2 litres/2 pints of the liquid. Shred the meat from the chicken, and shell and chop the prawns.

3 Heat 2 tablespoons of oil in a saucepan, add the spice paste and fry for a few seconds. Stir in 300ml/½ pint of the reserved liquid, the soy sauce, chicken and prawns. Simmer for 10 minutes. Add the remaining liquid and simmer for a further 10 minutes. Add the beansprouts and cook for 3 minutes.

2 Put the macadamias, shallots, garlic and ginger in a blender or food processor and blend to a purée. Add the turmeric and chilli powder and mix well. Alternatively, pound in a mortar.

1.5 litres/2½ pints water
1 x 1.25kg/2½lb chicken, quartered
4 uncooked king prawns
salt and freshly ground black pepper
2 macadamia nuts, chopped
4 shallots, chopped
2 garlic cloves, crushed
2 teaspoons grated root ginger
pinch of turmeric
pinch of chilli powder
vegetable oil for shallow-frying
1 tablespoon light soy sauce
75g/3oz beansprouts
1 potato, peeled and thinly sliced

PREPARATION: 20 MINUTES
COOKING: 1¼ HOURS
SERVES: 4-6

4 Meanwhile, fry the potato slices in some hot oil until golden and crisp. Remove and drain on absorbent kitchen paper. Serve the hot soup garnished with the fried potato.

INDIAN SPLIT PEA SOUP

Sarki

1 Pick over the yellow split peas to remove any grit and then wash under running cold water and drain them in a colander.

2 Put the drained split peas in a large saucepan with the water and turmeric, and bring to the boil. Reduce the heat and cover the pan. Simmer very gently for 1¼-1½ hours, until cooked and tender. Remove from the heat.

PREPARATION: 15 MINUTES +
CHILLING TIME
COOKING: 1¼ - 1½ HOURS
SERVES: 4

3 Put the split peas and their liquid in a large blender or food processor. Add the lemon juice, seasoning, chilli, cumin and coriander seeds, and blend until smooth. If the soup is a little too thick, thin it down with water or more lemon juice. Transfer to a serving bowl and refrigerate until required.

250g/8oz yellow split peas
1.3 litres/2¼ pints water
½ teaspoon turmeric
juice of ½ lemon
salt and freshly ground black pepper
1 fresh green chilli, seeded and finely chopped
1 teaspoon ground cumin
1 teaspoon ground coriander seeds
½ small cucumber
3 spring onions
75ml/3 fl oz yogurt
fresh mint leaves, to garnish

4 Just before serving, dice the cucumber and slice the spring onions. Swirl the yogurt into the chilled soup and serve garnished with the cucumber, spring onions and mint.

SPICED PEA SOUP

Hara shorva

25g/1oz ghee or butter
1 large onion, coarsely chopped
2 garlic cloves, chopped
1 small potato, diced
2.5cm/1 inch piece root ginger, peeled and sliced
1 teaspoon ground cumin seeds
1 teaspoon ground coriander seeds
900ml/1½ pints vegetable stock
250g/8oz fresh or frozen peas
1 fresh green chilli, chopped
salt and freshly ground black pepper
300ml/½ pint single cream
fresh coriander leaves, to garnish

3 Pour in the vegetable stock and bring to the boil. Reduce the heat, cover the pan and simmer gently for 15 minutes. Add the peas and chilli, and season to taste with salt and pepper. Continue cooking for 5 minutes over low heat.

1 Heat the ghee or butter in a large, heavy-based saucepan, and fry the onion and garlic gently for about 5 minutes, until soft and golden.

PREPARATION: 15 MINUTES
COOKING: 35-40 MINUTES
SERVES: 4

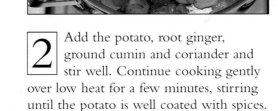

2 Add the potato, root ginger, ground cumin and coriander and stir well. Continue cooking gently over low heat for a few minutes, stirring until the potato is well coated with spices.

4 Blend the soup in a food processor or blender until smooth and return to the pan. Place over low heat and stir in the cream. Serve hot, garnished with coriander leaves.

MINCED MEAT SAMOSAS

Keema samosa

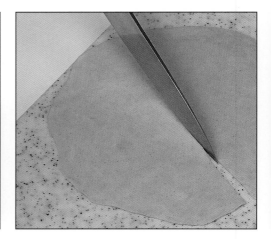

1 Make the filling: melt the butter in a saucepan, and fry the onion and cumin seeds over moderate heat, stirring occasionally, for 5-7 minutes. Add the minced beef, chilli and salt and mix thoroughly. Reduce the heat and simmer for 10 minutes.

2 Stir in the peas and continue cooking over moderate heat for 5 minutes, or until the liquid has evaporated. Remove the pan from the heat and mix in the pepper and coriander. Leave to cool before using to stuff the samosas.

3 Divide the samosa dough into 12 equal portions, and roll out each one to a thin 18cm/7-inch diameter circle. Cut each circle in half with a sharp knife, and then cover the semi-circles with a damp cloth while you fill them, one at a time.

1 quantity basic Samosa Dough (see page 110)
2 tablespoons milk
oil for deep-frying
chutney, to serve
For the filling:
1 tablespoon butter
1 small onion, chopped
1/2 teaspoon cumin seeds
250g/8oz minced beef
1 green chilli, finely chopped
1 teaspoon salt
125g/4oz cooked peas
pinch of freshly ground black pepper
1 teaspoon chopped coriander leaves

PREPARATION: 1 HOUR
(INCLUDING MAKING DOUGH)
COOKING: 25-30 MINUTES
SERVES: 6

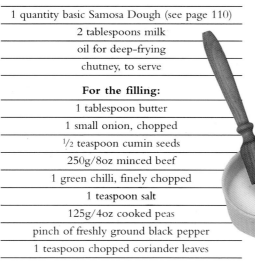

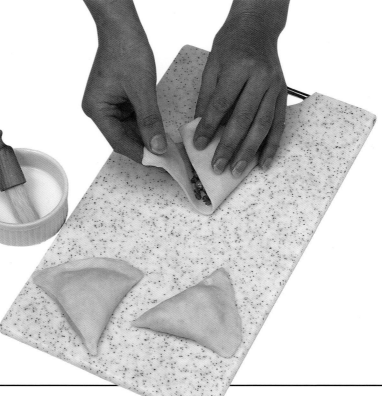

4 Brush the edges of each semi-circle with a little milk and spoon some filling on to the centre. Fold in the corners, overlapping them to form a cone. Fold over and seal the top to make a triangle. Deep-fry in hot oil, in batches, until crisp and golden. Drain on kitchen paper and serve hot, garnished with coriander sprigs.

VEGETABLE SAMOSAS

Aloo samosa

1 Make the filling: heat the ghee in a frying pan and add the asafoetida powder, mustard seeds, potatoes, peas, chillies, salt and pomegranate seeds, if using. Stir well over moderate heat for 2 minutes. Cover the pan, reduce the heat and cook gently for 10 minutes.

2 Remove the pan from the heat and add the garam masala and chopped coriander. Stir well and then leave the filling to cool before using to stuff the samosas.

4 Heat the oil for deep-frying and then fry the samosas, a few at a time, until crisp and golden. Remove with a slotted spoon and drain on absorbent kitchen paper. Serve them hot with your favourite chutney, garnished with coriander.

1 quantity basic Samosa Dough (see page 110)
2 tablespoons milk
oil for deep-frying
chutney, to serve
For the filling:
1 tablespoon ghee
pinch of asafoetida powder
2 teaspoons mustard seeds
500g/1lb potatoes, parboiled and diced
125g/4oz cooked peas
2 green chillies, seeded and chopped
1 teaspoon salt
1 teaspoon pomegranate seeds (optional)
1 teaspoon garam masala
2 tablespoons chopped coriander leaves

3 Roll out the samosa dough and prepare the semi-circles as described on page 18. Use the vegetable filling to stuff the samosas, and fold over (see page 18), sealing the edges with milk. Remember to cover them with a damp cloth while you are assembling them.

PREPARATION: 1 HOUR
(INCLUDING MAKING DOUGH)
COOKING: 20-25 MINUTES
SERVES: 6

SPICED FRIED PRAWNS

Jhinga

1 Remove the heads and shells from the prawns, leaving the tails intact. Carefully remove the black vein that runs along the back of each prawn.

3 Meanwhile, make the batter. Put the flour in a bowl and gradually add the water. Add a little salt and pepper, and then beat in the egg. Beat lightly until the batter is smooth and free from lumps.

500g/1lb cooked prawns
2 tablespoons tamarind water
pinch of turmeric
1 teaspoon grated root ginger
2 shallots or ¹/₂ onion, sliced
2 garlic cloves, crushed
1 tablespoon light soy sauce
150ml/¹/₄ pint oil for frying

For the batter:
75g/3oz rice flour or plain flour
4 tablespoons water
salt and pepper
1 small egg, beaten

PREPARATION: 15 MINUTES +
30 MINUTES MARINATING
COOKING: 10 MINUTES
SERVES: 4

2 Place the prawns in a bowl with the tamarind water, turmeric, ginger, shallots, garlic and soy sauce. Stir well and set aside to marinate in a cool place for 30 minutes.

4 Drain the marinade from the prawns and shallots, and then dip them into the batter. Heat the oil in a frying pan or wok and fry the prawns and shallots, in batches, until crisp and golden on both sides. Remove and drain on absorbent kitchen paper. Serve hot with plain boiled rice or some hot sauce or chutney.

INDIAN VEGETABLE FRITTERS

Pakoras

1 Make the batter: sift the flour into a bowl, rubbing any lumps through the sieve with the back of a spoon. Add the chilli powder and salt and mix well.

2 Gradually stir in the yogurt and lemon juice. Cover the bowl and leave to stand in a cool place for 2 hours, by which time the batter should be very thick.

PREPARATION: 20 MINUTES +
2 HOURS STANDING TIME
COOKING: 10 MINUTES
SERVES: 4

3 Dip the prepared vegetable pieces into the batter. They should be thoroughly coated all over. Heat the oil for deep-frying in a heavy saucepan or deep-fat fryer.

150g/5oz gram flour
1/2 teaspoon chilli powder
1/2 teaspoon salt
150ml/1/4 pint natural yogurt
1 teaspoon lemon juice
vegetable oil for deep-frying
For the filling:
375g/12oz chopped mixed vegetables, e.g. cauliflower florets, cubed aubergine, chopped green peppers and courgettes

4 Fry the pakoras, a few at a time, in the hot oil until golden and crisp, turning them carefully during cooking. Remove with a slotted spoon and drain on absorbent kitchen paper. Serve warm with chutney or a hot sauce of your choice.

FISH IN COCONUT MILK

Doodhia machhli

2 cloves, ground

4 green cardamoms, ground

2 fresh green chillies, crushed

2 garlic cloves, crushed

1cm/½ inch piece of root ginger, peeled and chopped

1 tablespoon Vindaloo Masala (see page 110)

salt

lemon juice

500g/1lb white fish fillets, e.g. sole or plaice

2 tablespoons mustard or vegetable oil

1 onion, thinly sliced

300ml/½ pint coconut milk

coriander sprigs, to garnish

2 Wash the fish fillets and pat them dry with absorbent kitchen paper. Spread the prepared spicy paste thickly and evenly over the fish.

1 In a bowl, mix together the cloves, cardamoms, chillies, garlic, ginger, Vindaloo masala powder and a little salt. Stir in enough lemon juice to make a smooth, thick paste.

PREPARATION: 20 MINUTES
COOKING: 30 MINUTES
SERVES: 4

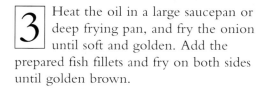

3 Heat the oil in a large saucepan or deep frying pan, and fry the onion until soft and golden. Add the prepared fish fillets and fry on both sides until golden brown.

4 Pour in the coconut milk and season to taste with salt. Cover the pan and cook gently over low heat for 15 minutes. Serve the fish sprinkled with coriander.

CURRIED FISH BALLS
Muchlikari

1 Put the fish fillets in an ovenproof dish and sprinkle with lemon juice. Cover with foil and stand in a roasting pan half-filled with water. Poach in a preheated oven at 160°C/325°F/Gas Mark 3 for 15 minutes. Remove and, when cool, flake the fish.

2 Whisk the egg with 1¹/₂ teaspoons of salt and some pepper. Sift in the chickpea flour, whisking all the time until the batter is smooth.

PREPARATION: 40 MINUTES
COOKING: 50-55 MINUTES
SERVES: 4

3 Add the flaked fish, chillies, onion and breadcrumbs to the batter. Stir well to make a stiff paste. Break off lumps and form into about 20 small balls. Heat the oil in a frying pan and shallow-fry the balls in batches until evenly browned. Drain and keep warm.

750g/1¹/₂lb white fish fillets, e.g. haddock or cod
juice of ¹/₂ lemon
1 egg
2¹/₂ teaspoons salt
freshly ground black pepper
50g/2oz chickpea flour (besan)
4 fresh green chillies, seeded and chopped
1 onion, finely chopped
2 tablespoons breadcrumbs
vegetable oil for shallow-frying
For the sauce:
125g/4oz ghee
1 large onion, thinly sliced
2 garlic cloves, thinly sliced
1 cinnamon stick
2 bay leaves
2 teaspoons each ground cumin and coriander
1¹/₂ teaspoons turmeric
1 teaspoon chilli powder
150g/5oz tomato paste
600ml/1 pint fish stock
juice of ¹/₂ lemon
50g/2oz desiccated coconut
seeds of 10 cardamoms, ground
2 teaspoons fenugreek seeds, ground

4 Make the sauce: melt the ghee and fry the onion and garlic for 5 minutes, until soft. Add all the spices and cook for 2 minutes. Add the tomato paste and bring to the boil. Add the remaining ingredients and cook over medium heat for 10 minutes. Add the fish balls, simmer for 5 minutes and serve hot with rice.

CHARCOAL-GRILLED FISH

Tandoori muchli

1 x 1-1.5kg/2-3lb halibut, cleaned and dried

juice of 1 lemon

2 teaspoons salt

1½ teaspoons freshly ground black pepper

For the masala:

1 large onion, peeled

1 garlic clove, peeled

1 tablespoon chopped fresh coriander leaves

4 teaspoons natural yogurt

2 teaspoons garam masala

1 teaspoon chilli powder

1 teaspoon ground coriander

1 teaspoon ground cumin

1 teaspoon ground fenugreek

2 Make the masala: put the onion and garlic in a food processor and chop finely. Alternatively, chop very finely with a knife or grate them on a grater.

3 Place the onion and garlic in a bowl with the coriander, yogurt, garam masala, chilli powder, ground coriander, cumin and fenugreek, and mix well.

4 Smear this mixture over the fish and inside the cuts and the cavity. Draw up the sides of the foil to make a tent shape and seal the edges. Leave in a cool place to marinate for 4 hours. Bake in a preheated oven at 160°C/325°F/Gas Mark 3 for 20 minutes. Remove the fish carefully and finish cooking on a barbecue or on a wire rack in the oven.

1 Line a large baking dish with a sheet of foil 2½ times the size of the fish. Make 4 or 5 deep cuts in each side of the fish. Rub the fish with lemon juice and sprinkle with salt and pepper. Place the fish on the foil and set aside.

PREPARATION: 15 MINUTES
+ 4 HOURS MARINATING
COOKING: 25-30 MINUTES
SERVES: 4

FISH TANDOORI

Myhee tandoori

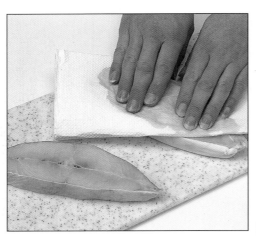

1 Wash the halibut steaks under cold running water, and then gently pat them dry with absorbent kitchen paper. Set aside while you prepare the tandoori mixture.

3 Place the halibut steaks in the bowl and rub well with the tandoori mixture. Cover the bowl and leave in a cool place to marinate for 4-5 hours.

| 4 halibut steaks, about 175g/6oz each |
| 50g/2oz natural yogurt |
| 2 tablespoons oil |
| 2 tablespoons paprika |
| 1 tablespoon ground cumin |
| 1 teaspoon ground fennel seeds |
| 1 teaspoon chilli powder |
| salt |
| **To garnish:** |
| 1 small lettuce, shredded |
| 1 fennel bulb, sliced |
| lemon wedges |

2 Put the yogurt in a bowl with the oil, paprika, cumin, fennel seeds, chilli powder and a little salt. Mix well together.

4 Transfer the marinated fish to a shallow, ovenproof baking dish. Bake uncovered in a preheated oven at 180°C/350°F/Gas Mark 4 for 20-25 minutes. Arrange the lettuce and fennel on a warm serving dish and place the fish on top. Spoon over the juices and serve, garnished with lemon.

PREPARATION: 15 MINUTES
+ 4-5 HOURS MARINATING
COOKING: 20-25 MINUTES
SERVES: 4

FISH KEBABS

Kabab tikkah Machchi

1 Put the ginger, garlic, cumin, black pepper, coriander, garam masala, cloves and aniseed in a large bowl. Stir in the yogurt and mix together until well blended.

3 Peel the onions and cut them into thick slices. Thread them onto some wooden kebab skewers, alternating with the marinated fish.

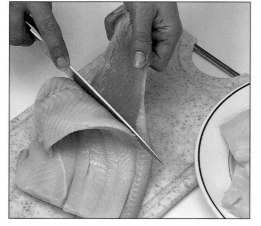

2 Remove the skin from the fish fillets and wash them. Pat dry with absorbent kitchen paper and then cut the fillets into cubes. Add them to the yogurt mixture and turn to coat. Leave to marinate in a cool place for at least 1 hour.

4 Brush the kebabs with any remaining yogurt marinade and a little oil. Arrange on a grill pan and place under a preheated grill until cooked and lightly browned all over. Turn the kebabs occasionally and baste with oil and marinade as necessary. Serve with lime wedges and yogurt raita, scattered with mint sprigs.

5cm/2 inch piece of root ginger, peeled and crushed
1 garlic clove, crushed
2 teaspoons ground cumin
1 teaspoon freshly ground black pepper
1 teaspoon ground coriander
1 teaspoon garam masala
$\frac{1}{2}$ teaspoon ground cloves
1 teaspoon ground aniseed
75ml/3 fl oz natural yogurt
1kg/2lb white fish fillets
4 small onions
oil for basting
To serve:
lime wedges
yogurt raita (see page 110)

PREPARATION: 15 MINUTES +
MARINATING TIME
COOKING: 10-15 MINUTES
SERVES: 4

PRAWN CURRY

Jhinga kari

1 Melt the ghee in a large, heavy-based saucepan. Add the onion and garlic and fry gently over low heat for 4-5 minutes, until golden and soft.

2 In a small bowl, mix together the ground coriander, ginger, turmeric, cumin and chilli powder. Mix in the vinegar to make a smooth paste.

3 Add the spicy paste to the onion and garlic mixture in the pan, and then fry gently for a further 3 minutes, stirring constantly with a wooden spoon.

50g/2oz ghee
1 small onion, sliced
2 garlic cloves, sliced
2 teaspoons ground coriander
1/2 teaspoon ground ginger
1 teaspoon turmeric
1/2 teaspoon ground cumin
1/2 teaspoon chilli powder
2 tablespoons vinegar
500g/1lb peeled prawns
200ml/7 fl oz water
chopped fresh coriander leaves, to garnish

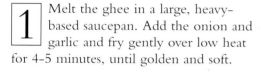

4 Add the prawns and turn gently with a wooden spoon until they are well coated with the spices. Stir in the water and then simmer over gentle heat for 2-3 minutes. Serve immediately, garnished with coriander leaves, with plain boiled rice.

PREPARATION: 15 MINUTES
COOKING: 12-15 MINUTES
SERVES: 4

BARBECUED KING PRAWNS
Tandoori jhinga

1 Wash the prawns and remove the heads. Make a slit along the underside of each shell with a sharp knife and then slightly flatten them. Place in a bowl and sprinkle with the lemon juice, salt and pepper. Mix well and then set aside.

2 Make the marinade: spread the coriander, fenugreek, cardamom and black onion seeds on a baking tray. Add the bay leaves and place in a preheated oven at 200°C/400°F/Gas Mark 6 for 10-15 minutes. Remove and cool, then grind with a mortar and pestle.

3 Place the onion, garlic and ginger in a blender or food processor with the yogurt and turmeric, and blend until smooth. Add the ground roasted spices and ghee and blend again for 30 seconds. Add the food colouring.

1kg/2lb king prawns
juice of 2 lemons
1½ teaspoons salt
1½ teaspoons freshly ground black pepper
1 teaspoon aniseed
For the marinade:
2 teaspoons coriander seeds
2 teaspoons fenugreek seeds
seeds of 20 cardamoms
1½ teaspoons black onion seeds (kalonji)
4 bay leaves
1 large **onion**, chopped
3 garlic cloves, chopped
7.5cm/3 inch piece of root ginger, peeled and chopped
350ml/12 fl oz natural yogurt
1½ teaspoons turmeric
125g/4oz ghee, melted
few drops of red food colouring

4 Pour the marinade over the prawns, cover and marinate in the refrigerator for 6-8 hours or over-night. Remove the prawns and thread on to skewers. Sprinkle with aniseed and barbecue (or grill) gently for about 5 minutes, turning frequently and brushing with the marinade. Serve hot.

PREPARATION: 30 MINUTES
+ 6-8 HOURS MARINATING
COOKING: 15-20 MINUTES
SERVES: 4

SPICY STEAMED MUSSELS

Teesryo

1 Scrub the mussels under cold running water and remove the beards. Place in a large bowl, cover with fresh cold water and leave to soak for 20-30 minutes.

1kg/2lb fresh mussels
125g/4oz ghee
1 large onion, finely chopped
2 garlic cloves, finely chopped
2 teaspoons desiccated coconut
2 teaspoons salt
1 teaspoon turmeric
1 teaspoon chilli powder
1 teaspoon freshly ground black pepper
150ml/¼ pint vinegar
500ml/17 fl oz natural yogurt
2 teaspoons garam masala
juice of 2 lemons
coriander sprigs, to garnish

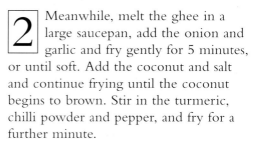

2 Meanwhile, melt the ghee in a large saucepan, add the onion and garlic and fry gently for 5 minutes, or until soft. Add the coconut and salt and continue frying until the coconut begins to brown. Stir in the turmeric, chilli powder and pepper, and fry for a further minute.

3 Drain the mussels and discard any that are open. Add the vinegar and mussels to the pan, cover with a tight-fitting lid and turn up the heat. Cook over high heat for 5 minutes, shaking the pan occasionally, until the mussels open. Remove from the heat.

4 Arrange the mussels in layers in a warm serving dish. Pour the cooking liquid into a blender or food processor, add the yogurt and garam masala, and blend for 1 minute. Return to the pan and heat through without boiling. Pour the liquid over the mussels and serve, sprinkled with lemon juice and coriander sprigs.

PREPARATION: 20 MINUTES
+ SOAKING TIME
COOKING: 10-15 MINUTES
SERVES: 4

NUGGETS OF LAMB

Preeti kabab

1 In a large bowl, mix together the minced lamb, onion, garlic, chillies, coriander seeds and leaves, ginger, cumin seeds, bicarbonate of soda and salt.

1kg/2lb lean lamb, minced
1 medium onion, finely chopped
8 garlic cloves, crushed
4 fresh green chillies, finely chopped
1 tablespoon coriander seeds, ground
2 tablespoons chopped fresh coriander leaves
50g/2oz root ginger, grated
2 teaspoons cumin seeds
pinch of bicarbonate of soda
2½ teaspoons salt
2 egg whites
6 tablespoons vegetable oil
sauce or chutney, to serve

To garnish:

coriander leaves
lemon wedges

PREPARATION: 25 MINUTES
COOKING: 30 MINUTES
SERVES: 6

3 Put the egg whites in a clean, dry bowl and whisk until stiff. Dip the prepared nuggets into the beaten egg white to coat them.

2 Divide the minced lamb mixture into 18 equal portions, and then shape them into 'nuggets' between your hands.

4 Heat the oil in a large frying pan, 1 tablespoon at a time, and fry the nuggets in batches until they are all cooked through. Serve garnished with coriander leaves and lemon wedges, with a sauce or chutney of your choice.

LAMB KEBABS
Madhu kabab

750g/1½lb lean lamb, minced

1 teaspoon grated root ginger

1 large onion, finely chopped

25g/1oz gram flour

2 fresh green chillies, finely chopped

1 teaspoon green mango powder

1 tablespoon salt

2 tablespoons lemon juice

1 egg

2 tablespoons chopped coriander leaves

50g/2oz ghee, melted

For the spices:

½ teaspoon poppy seeds, roasted and ground

1 teaspoon garam masala

1 tablespoon yellow or red chilli powder

½ teaspoon freshly ground black pepper

1 teaspoon black cumin seeds, roasted and ground

1 tablespoon ground coriander seeds

To garnish:

lime wedges

2 Work the egg and chopped coriander into the minced meat mixture. Continue kneading the mixture until it becomes sticky.

3 Divide the minced meat mixture into 18 equal-sized portions, and then form each piece between your hands into a sausage shape.

1 Mix the minced meat, ginger, onion, gram flour, chillies, mango powder, salt and lemon juice together with all the spices. Set aside for 30 minutes to allow the flavours to develop.

PREPARATION:
30 MINUTES
+ 30 MINUTES STANDING TIME
COOKING: 20-30 MINUTES
SERVES: 6

4 Thread the 'sausages' on to skewers. For longer kebabs, flatten them out on the skewers. Cook under a preheated hot grill or over charcoal, turning frequently. Brush the kebabs with melted ghee while they are cooking. Serve hot, garnished with lime wedges.

LAMB WITH ALMONDS

Roganjosh

1 Make the masala: grind the ginger, garlic, mace, nutmeg, cloves, poppy seeds, peppercorns, almonds and cardamoms. Add a little water to make a fine paste.

2 Heat the ghee in a deep frying pan and gently fry the onion until light brown. Add the small green cardamoms and stir in the masala paste. Fry over low heat for 2 minutes.

3 Add the turmeric, chilli powder, cumin, paprika and coriander to the pan, and fry over gentle heat for a further 1–2 minutes.

50g/2oz ghee
125g/4oz finely chopped onion
5 small green cardamoms
1/2 teaspoon ground turmeric
1 teaspoon chilli powder
1 teaspoon ground cumin
1 1/2 teaspoons paprika
1 teaspoon ground coriander
150ml/1/4 pint natural yogurt
250g/8oz tomatoes, skinned and chopped
500g/1lb boned leg of lamb, cut into 2.5cm/1 inch cubes
chopped coriander leaves, to garnish

For the masala:
15g/1/2oz root ginger, peeled and chopped
6 garlic cloves, peeled
1 blade of mace
1/4 teaspoon ground nutmeg
4 cloves
1 tablespoon dry-roasted poppy seeds
12 peppercorns
50g/2oz blanched almonds
seeds of 2 large cardamoms

4 Stir in the yogurt and tomatoes, and then the lamb with a little salt. Cover and cook over low heat for 40–50 minutes, sprinkling with a little water if necessary. Serve garnished with coriander.

PREPARATION: 30 MINUTES
COOKING: 1 HOUR
SERVES: 4

MEATBALL CURRY

Kofta kari

500g/1lb minced beef

2 large onions, chopped

4 garlic cloves, crushed

2 teaspoons turmeric

2 teaspoons chilli powder

2 teaspoons ground coriander

1½ teaspoons ground cumin

1 teaspoon ground ginger

2 teaspoons salt

1 egg, beaten

vegetable oil for deep-frying

125g/4oz ghee

200ml/7 fl oz water

fresh mint or coriander leaves, to garnish

2 Divide the minced beef mixture into 12 equal-sized portions and, using your hands, shape each one into a small ball.

1 Put the minced beef in a bowl with half of the onions, garlic, spices and salt. Stir well and then bind the mixture together with the beaten egg.

PREPARATION: 30 MINUTES
COOKING: 50 MINUTES
SERVES: 4

3 Heat the oil in a heavy-based saucepan until it is very hot. Add the meatballs in batches and deep-fry for 5 minutes. Remove and drain on absorbent kitchen paper, and then set aside.

4 Melt the ghee in a large saucepan, add the remaining onions and garlic and fry gently for 4-5 minutes until soft. Add the remaining spices and salt and fry for 3 minutes, stirring. Add the meatballs and coat them in the spices. Add the water and bring to the boil. Lower the heat and simmer gently for 30 minutes. Serve garnished with mint or coriander leaves.

CALCUTTA BEEF CURRY
Calcutta gosht

1 Cut the beef into 4cm/1½ inch cubes, being careful to trim away any excess fat. Put the salt and ground spices, except the garam masala, in a large bowl. Mix in the milk, a little at a time.

2 Add the cubes of beef to the bowl and turn in the milk and spice mixture until they are evenly coated.

3 Melt the ghee in a large, heavy-based saucepan, add the onions, garlic and ginger and fry gently for 4-5 minutes until soft. Remove the beef from the milk and spice mixture and fry over moderate heat, turning constantly until evenly browned.

4 Increase the heat, add the milk and spice mixture and bring to the boil. Cover the pan, reduce the heat and cook gently for 1½-2 hours, until the beef is tender and the sauce reduced. Just before serving, add the garam masala and boil off any excess liquid to make a thick sauce.

| 1kg/2¼lb braising steak |
| 1 teaspoon salt |
| 1 tablespoon chilli powder |
| 2 teaspoons ground coriander |
| 1 teaspoon freshly ground black pepper |
| 1½ teaspoons turmeric |
| 1 teaspoon ground cumin |
| 1 litre/1¾ pints milk |
| 125g/4oz ghee |
| 2 large onions, thinly sliced |
| 5 garlic cloves, thinly sliced |
| 7.5cm/3 inch piece of root ginger, peeled and thinly sliced |
| 2 teaspoons garam masala |

PREPARATION: 15 MINUTES
COOKING: 1¾-2¼ HOURS
SERVES: 6

SPICY BEEF IN YOGURT
Pasanda

1 Place the beef between 2 sheets of greaseproof paper and beat until thin with a rolling pin or mallet.

2 Rub the beef with the salt, and then cut into serving-sized pieces. Place in a bowl and cover with the yogurt. Cover and leave to marinate overnight in the refrigerator.

PREPARATION: 15 MINUTES
+ MARINATING TIME
COOKING: 1¾ HOURS
SERVES: 4

3 Melt the ghee in a heavy-based saucepan, and add the onion and garlic. Fry gently for 4-5 minutes until soft. Add the spices and fry for a further 3 minutes, stirring constantly.

4 Add the beef and yogurt marinade to the pan and stir well. Cover the pan with a tightly fitting lid and then simmer for 1½ hours, or until the meat is tender. Serve with rice.

500g/1lb braising or stewing steak
1 teaspoon salt
300ml/½ pint natural yogurt
175g/6oz ghee
1 large onion, sliced
3 garlic cloves, sliced
1½ teaspoons ground ginger
2 teaspoons ground coriander
2 teaspoons chilli powder
½ teaspoon ground cumin
1½ teaspoons turmeric
1 teaspoon garam masala

CHICKEN BIRIYANI

Murgh biriani

1 Grind all the paste ingredients together in a mortar or food processor to make a smooth mixture. Rub this paste over the chicken drumsticks and leave them to marinate for 30 minutes.

8 chicken drumsticks
175g/6oz ghee
25g/1oz chopped almonds
25g/1oz chopped cashew nuts
1 large onion, finely chopped
1 quantity Biriyani Spices (see page 111)
4 bay leaves
425g/14oz long-grain rice
½ teaspoon saffron strands
2 tablespoons melted butter
chopped chilli and coriander, to garnish

For the paste:
1 teaspoon garam masala
1 small onion, chopped
2 garlic cloves, crushed
5cm/2 inch piece of root ginger
150ml/5 fl oz natural yogurt
1 teaspoon salt

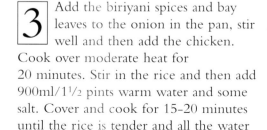

2 Heat the ghee in a frying pan and fry the almonds and cashews until golden brown. Remove with a slotted spoon and drain on absorbent kitchen paper. Set aside for the garnish. Add the onion to the pan and fry until golden. Remove half of it and keep for the garnish.

3 Add the biriyani spices and bay leaves to the onion in the pan, stir well and then add the chicken. Cook over moderate heat for 20 minutes. Stir in the rice and then add 900ml/1½ pints warm water and some salt. Cover and cook for 15-20 minutes until the rice is tender and all the water absorbed.

4 Steep the saffron in a little water for 5 minutes. Add the melted butter and then stir into the rice. Serve garnished with the reserved fried onions and nuts, chilli and coriander.

PREPARATION: 30 MINUTES
+ MARINATING TIME
COOKING: 50 MINUTES
SERVES: 4

CHICKEN KORMA

Kookarh korma

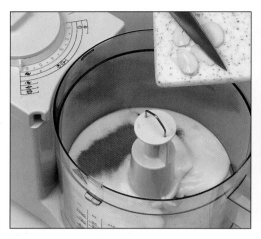

1 Put the yogurt, turmeric and one of the garlic cloves in a blender or food processor, and then blend to a smooth purée.

2 Place the chicken pieces in a shallow dish and pour the yogurt mixture over them. Cover the dish and leave to marinate in the refrigerator overnight.

3 Melt the ghee in a large, heavy-based saucepan, and add the onion and remaining garlic. Fry gently for 4–5 minutes until soft. Add the spices and salt and fry for a further 3 minutes, stirring constantly.

175ml/6 fl oz natural yogurt
2 teaspoons turmeric
3 garlic cloves, sliced
1 x 1.5kg/3lb roasting chicken, skinned and cut into 8 pieces
125g/4oz ghee
1 large onion, sliced
1 teaspoon ground ginger
5cm/2 inch cinnamon stick
5 cloves
5 cardamoms
1 tablespoon crushed coriander seeds
1 teaspoon ground cumin
1/2 teaspoon chilli powder
1 teaspoon salt
1 1/2 tablespoons desiccated coconut
2 teaspoons toasted almonds
coriander leaves, to garnish

PREPARATION: 15 MINUTES
+ MARINATING TIME
COOKING: 55 MINUTES
SERVES: 4

4 Add the chicken pieces with the yogurt marinade and coconut, and mix well. Cover the pan with a tightly fitting lid and then simmer gently for 45 minutes, or until the chicken is cooked and tender. Transfer to a warmed serving dish and scatter with the almonds and coriander.

Tandoori chicken

Murgh tandoori

1 Remove the skin from the chicken pieces and discard. Wash and dry the chicken, and then slash each piece several times with a sharp knife. Place in a large dish and sprinkle with lemon juice and salt. Rub this mixture in well, and then cover and leave in a cool place for 1 hour.

2 Meanwhile, prepare the marinade: spread the cloves, coriander, cumin and cardamom seeds on a baking tray and roast in a preheated oven at 200°C/400°F/Gas Mark 6 for 10-15 minutes. Remove and, when cool, grind them coarsely in a mortar.

PREPARATION: 45 MINUTES
+ STANDING + MARINATING TIME
COOKING: 35-40 MINUTES
SERVES: 8

3 Put the onions, garlic and ginger in a blender or food processor and sprinkle with the chilli powder, black pepper and turmeric. Add the yogurt and ground roasted spices and strain in the lemon juice from the chicken. Blend until smooth, adding some red food colouring if wished.

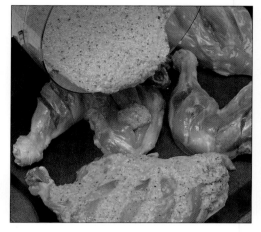

4 Place the chicken pieces in a single layer in a large roasting pan and pour over the marinade. Cover the pan and leave in the refrigerator to marinate for at least 24 hours, turning occasionally. Cook in a preheated oven at 200°C/400°F/Gas Mark 6 for 20 minutes and then place under a hot grill until crisp. Serve hot or cold.

8 chicken quarters
juice of 2 lemons
2 teaspoons salt
For the marinade:
10 cloves
2 teaspoons coriander seeds
2 teaspoons cumin seeds
seeds of 10 cardamoms
2 medium onions, chopped
4 garlic cloves, chopped
7.5cm/3 inch piece root ginger, peeled and chopped
2 teaspoons chilli powder
2 teaspoons freshly ground black pepper
1½ teaspoons turmeric
350ml/12 fl oz natural yogurt
few drops of red food colouring (optional)

CHICKEN VINDALOO

Murghi vindaloo

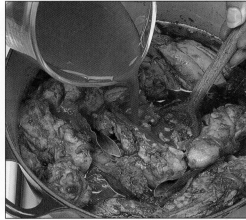

1 Put the vindaloo masala, vinegar and 2 teaspoons of salt in a bowl and then mix well to make a smooth paste.

2 Wash and dry the chicken pieces and make a few deep gashes in each one with a sharp knife. Rub the paste all over them and leave in a cool place to marinate for 1 hour.

2 tablespoons Vindaloo Masala (see page 110)
2 teaspoons vinegar
salt
1 x 1.5kg/3lb chicken, cut into pieces
6 tablespoons mustard or vegetable oil
4 bay leaves
1 teaspoon green cardamom seeds
1 large onion, thinly sliced
2 teaspoons turmeric powder
1 teaspoon cayenne pepper
10 garlic cloves, crushed
15g/½ oz root ginger, peeled and thinly sliced
2 tomatoes, skinned and quartered
150ml/¼ pint tamarind juice or water
2 teaspoons desiccated coconut

3 Heat the mustard oil in a large saucepan and stir in the bay leaves and cardamom seeds. Add the onion and fry until light brown. Stir in the turmeric and cayenne pepper and add the chicken pieces. Cook, stirring occasionally, for 15 minutes. Add 1 teaspoon of salt, the garlic, ginger and tomatoes and cook for 10 minutes, stirring.

4 When the fat starts to separate, add the tamarind juice or water. Stir well, cover the pan and simmer gently for about 25 minutes, or until the chicken is tender. Sprinkle with desiccated coconut and serve.

PREPARATION: 15 MINUTES
+ MARINATING TIME
COOKING: 55 MINUTES
SERVES: 6

CHICKEN WITH LENTILS

Murgh dhansak

500g/1lb dried split peas or lentils,
e.g. moong dhal

1.2 litres/2 pints water

175g/6oz ghee

2 large onions, sliced

4 garlic cloves, sliced

6 cloves

6 cardamoms

1½ teaspoons ground ginger

2 teaspoons garam masala

2½ teaspoons salt

1 x 1.5kg/3lb chicken, skinned,
boned and cut into 8 pieces

500g/1lb frozen whole-leaf spinach

4 large tomatoes, skinned and chopped

1 Wash the split peas or lentils and then place in a large saucepan. Add the water and bring to the boil. Cover the pan, lower the heat and simmer for 15 minutes.

PREPARATION: 30 MINUTES
COOKING: 1¼ HOURS
SERVES: 4

2 Meanwhile, melt the ghee in a large, heavy-based saucepan, add the onions and garlic and fry for 4-5 minutes until soft. Add the spices and salt and fry for 3 minutes, stirring constantly. Add the chicken and brown on all sides, and then remove and drain on absorbent kitchen paper.

3 Add the spinach and tomatoes to the saucepan and fry gently over low heat for 10 minutes, stirring occasionally.

4 Mash the peas or lentils in their cooking water, and then stir them into the spinach mixture. Return the chicken to the pan, cover with a tightly fitting lid and simmer gently for 45 minutes, or until the chicken is cooked and tender.

ROAST CHICKEN WITH ALMONDS

Moghlai murgh

1 Heat the oil and 50g/2oz of the ghee in a frying pan and add the onions. Fry until golden brown. Mix in the saffron and yogurt, and set aside to cool.

2 Put the coriander and cumin seeds with the salt, pepper, cloves and cardamoms in a mortar, and pound well. Rub this spice mixture all over the chicken and place in a roasting pan.

PREPARATION: 20 MINUTES
COOKING: 1¼ HOURS
SERVES: 4-6

3 Put the chicken in a preheated oven at 190°C/375°F/Gas Mark 5 for about 1¼ hours, until the chicken is cooked and tender. After about 20 minutes, baste the chicken with the yogurt mixture and return to the oven. Keep basting the chicken at regular intervals.

2 tablespoons oil
75g/3oz ghee
3 onions, chopped
good pinch of ground saffron
300ml/½ pint natural yogurt
1 tablespoon coriander seeds
1 teaspoon cumin seeds
salt and freshly ground black pepper
8 cloves
6 whole cardamoms
1 x 1.5kg/3lb roasting chicken
125g/4oz blanched slivered almonds
50g/2oz raisins

4 While the chicken is cooking, fry the almonds in the remaining ghee until they start to turn golden brown. Add the raisins and stir well. Remove from the heat. Serve the chicken, topped with the almonds and raisins, with some plain boiled rice.

SAFFRON RICE

Kesari chawal

1 Put the saffron threads in a small bowl with the boiling water and leave to soak for 30 minutes. Melt the ghee in a large, heavy-based saucepan and then add the onions. Fry gently for 4-5 minutes until soft.

2 Put the rice in a sieve and wash thoroughly under cold running water to remove any milling and polishing dust. Drain well.

3 Add the rice to the onions in the pan, and then stir in the cloves, cardamoms, salt and pepper. Fry for 3 minutes, stirring frequently.

| ½ teaspoon saffron threads |
| 1 tablespoon boiling water |
| 175g/6oz ghee |
| 2 large onions, sliced |
| 375g/12oz Basmati or Patna rice |
| 1 teaspoon cloves |
| 4 cardamoms |
| 1 teaspoon salt |
| 1 teaspoon freshly ground black pepper |
| 750ml/1¼ pints water |
| silver leaf (varak), to garnish (optional) |

4 Meanwhile, put the water in a kettle and bring to the boil. Add to the pan, together with the saffron and its soaking liquid, then lower the heat and simmer for 15-20 minutes until the rice is cooked. Drain well and transfer the rice to a serving dish. Serve hot, garnished, if liked, with silver leaf.

PREPARATION: 15 MINUTES
+ SOAKING TIME
COOKING: 30-35 MINUTES
SERVES: 4

VEGETABLE BIRIYANI

Sabziyon ki biriyani

1 Heat the ghee or oil in a large saucepan and fry the onion until golden. Remove half of the fried onion and set aside for the garnish. Add the garlic and spices to the pan and fry for 2-3 minutes.

2 Rinse the rice in several changes of water and then drain well. Add to the pan and stir well. Cook for a further 5 minutes until all the grains are glistening and translucent.

3 Add the mixed diced vegetables and salt together with the stock, and bring to the boil. Cover the pan and reduce the heat to a bare simmer. Cook gently for 20-25 minutes, until all the liquid has been absorbed and the rice is cooked.

3 tablespoons ghee or vegetable oil
1 large onion, finely chopped
2 garlic cloves, chopped
8 cloves
2 x 2.5cm/1 inch cinnamon sticks
4 green cardamom pods
1 teaspoon turmeric
1 teaspoon garam masala
500g/1lb Basmati rice, pre-soaked
250g/8oz mixed diced vegetables, e.g. carrots, cauliflower, courgettes, okra, peas
salt
600ml/1 pint vegetable stock
50g/2oz paneer, lightly fried (see page 111)
125g/4oz chopped mixed nuts, e.g. almonds, cashews, pistachios
50g/2oz sultanas

PREPARATION: 15 MINUTES
COOKING: 40-45 MINUTES
SERVES: 4-6

4 Add the paneer, nuts and sultanas, and mix well. Cover and cook for 5 minutes over low heat until all the moisture has evaporated. Serve hot, sprinkled with the reserved fried onion.

RICE WITH VEGETABLES

Subzi pilao

1 Mix the vegetables together and set aside. Mix together the ground spices and salt. Melt half of the ghee in a large saucepan, then add half of the spice mixture and fry gently for 2 minutes. Stir in the vegetables to coat with the spices and then remove and keep warm.

2 Melt the remaining ghee in the saucepan and add the onions, garlic and ginger. Fry gently for 5 minutes until soft. Add the cinnamon sticks, cardamoms, cloves and lovage seeds and fry for 3-4 minutes. Add the remaining spice mixture and fry for 2 minutes.

3 Wash and drain the rice. Add to the saucepan and stir until the grains are coated with the spices. Pour in 2 litres/3½ pints boiling water and boil, uncovered, until the rice is cooked but firm. Stir to prevent the rice sticking, adding more water if necessary.

4 When the rice is ready, drain it in a large sieve. Mix with the reserved vegetables and serve scattered with sultanas and almonds.

250g/8oz blanched diced mixed vegetables
125g/4oz blanched diced red and green peppers
125g/4oz courgettes, trimmed and diced
2 tablespoons ground cumin
2 tablespoons ground coriander
1 tablespoon chilli powder
2 teaspoons turmeric
4 teaspoons black peppercorns, crushed
2 teaspoons salt
125g/4oz ghee
4 large onions, thinly sliced
5 garlic cloves, thinly sliced
2 x 7.5cm/3 inch pieces of root ginger, peeled and sliced
2 x 7.5cm/3 inch cinnamon sticks
20 cardamoms
20 cloves
1 tablespoon lovage seeds (optional)
750g/1½lb Basmati rice
75g/3oz sultanas
50g/2oz flaked almonds

PREPARATION:
15 MINUTES
COOKING:
35-40 MINUTES
SERVES: 6-8

CHICKEN PILAU

Murghi pilau

375g/12oz Basmati rice

5 tablespoons ghee

5cm/2 inch cinnamon stick

8 cloves

6 cardamom seeds

2 garlic cloves, crushed

1 teaspoon chilli powder

1 tablespoon fennel seeds

4 chicken portions, skinned

5 tablespoons natural yogurt

1 teaspoon powdered saffron

1½ teaspoons salt

600ml/1 pint chicken stock

To garnish:

2 large onions, sliced

4 tablespoons ghee

coriander leaves

3 Add the chicken portions and fry, turning occasionally, for 5 minutes. Stir in the yogurt, a spoonful at a time, and then cover the pan and simmer for 25 minutes.

1 Wash the rice thoroughly and drain. Place in a large bowl and cover with fresh cold water. Leave to soak for 30 minutes, and then drain well.

PREPARATION: 20 MINUTES
+ SOAKING TIME
COOKING: ABOUT 1 HOUR
SERVES: 4

2 Melt the ghee in a large saucepan and add the cinnamon, cloves and cardamom seeds. Fry briskly for 30 seconds and then stir in the garlic, chilli powder and fennel seeds. Fry for a further 30 seconds.

4 Add the rice, saffron and salt. Fry, stirring, until the rice is glistening and coated with spices. Add enough stock to cover the rice by 5mm/¼ inch and bring to the boil. Reduce the heat to a simmer and cook, covered tightly, for 20 minutes or until the rice is cooked. In another pan, fry the onions in the ghee. Use to garnish the pilau along with the coriander.

KITCHEREE

Bhooni kitcheri

1 Mix the rice and lentils together and then wash thoroughly in cold water. Drain well, place in a bowl and cover with fresh cold water and leave to soak for 1 hour.

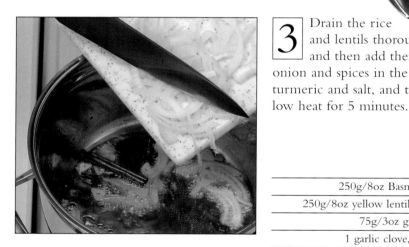

2 Heat the ghee in a large pan and fry the garlic, cloves, cardamom and cinnamon for 1 minute. Add the onion and fry for 1-2 minutes.

PREPARATION: 15 MINUTES
+ SOAKING TIME
COOKING: 40-55 MINUTES
SERVES: 4

3 Drain the rice and lentils thoroughly and then add them to the onion and spices in the pan. Stir in the turmeric and salt, and toss gently over low heat for 5 minutes.

250g/8oz Basmati rice
250g/8oz yellow lentils (moong dhal)
75g/3oz ghee
1 garlic clove, sliced
5 cloves
5 cardamom seeds
5cm/2 inch piece cinnamon stick
1 small onion, sliced
1 teaspoon turmeric
½ teaspoon salt
To garnish:
fried onion rings
chopped fresh coriander leaves

4 Add enough boiling water to cover the rice by 2.5cm/1 inch, and then cover the pan with a tightly fitting lid. Simmer over low heat for 30-45 minutes until the rice is cooked and the liquid absorbed. Serve garnished with fried onion rings and chopped coriander.

PRAWN AND SPINACH RICE
Machachi pilau

1 Place the Basmati rice in a sieve and wash thoroughly under cold running water. Drain well. Fill a large saucepan two-thirds full with water and bring to the boil. Add the rice with 1 teaspoon of salt and the turmeric. Boil the rice for 3 minutes and then drain. Stir in the butter.

4 Layer the spinach mixture with the buttered rice in an ovenproof casserole dish, beginning and ending with the spinach. Cover tightly and cook in a preheated oven at 180°C/350°F/Gas Mark 4 for 30 minutes. Serve immediately.

2 Heat the oil in a large saucepan and add the onions, garlic and ginger. Fry for 5 minutes until golden. Stir in the chilli powder, coriander and 1 teaspoon of salt, and fry for a few seconds.

3 Add the washed and chopped spinach and cook, stirring constantly, until softened. Stir in the prawns and then remove from the heat.

| 500g/1lb Basmati rice |
| salt |
| ½ teaspoon turmeric |
| 50g/2oz butter |
| 3 tablespoons oil |
| 2 onions, sliced |
| 3 garlic cloves, finely chopped |
| 1 tablespoon grated root ginger |
| 1-2 teaspoons chilli powder |
| 2 teaspoons ground coriander |
| 1kg/2lb spinach, washed, trimmed and chopped |
| 500g/1lb cooked peeled prawns |

PREPARATION: 30 MINUTES
COOKING: 30 MINUTES
SERVES: 4

GRAM AND BEAN DHAL

Chana urad dall

1 Put 1.2 litres/2 pints of water into a large saucepan and bring to the boil. Meanwhile, wash the grams and beans in a colander under cold running water, and then drain well.

3 Cut the marrow into 5cm/2 inch pieces and add to the saucepan with the grams and beans. Simmer gently for a further 30 minutes.

2 Tip the drained grams and beans into the boiling water with the salt and turmeric. Bring the water back to the boil, cover the pan and simmer for 1½ hours, stirring occasionally.

125g/4oz split grams or yellow split peas
125g/4oz dried beans
good pinch of salt
½ teaspoon turmeric powder
125g/4oz peeled and sliced marrow
125g/4oz ghee
1 onion, finely chopped
6 garlic cloves, crushed
1 teaspoon white cumin seeds
1 fresh green chilli, chopped
1 dry red chilli, crushed
½ teaspoon chilli powder

4 Heat the ghee in a frying pan and fry the onion, garlic and cumin until golden brown. Remove from the heat and add the chopped chillies and chilli powder. Transfer the dhal to a small serving bowl. Serve hot with the spiced fried onion sprinkled on top.

PREPARATION: 15 MINUTES
COOKING: ABOUT 2 HOURS
SERVES: 6

FRIED CHILLI CABBAGE
Bandhgobi

125g/4oz ghee
1 small onion, chopped
6 garlic cloves, crushed
1 teaspoon white cumin seeds
1 teaspoon turmeric powder
1 medium white cabbage, coarsely chopped
125g/4oz potatoes, peeled and chopped
125g/4oz shelled peas
125g/4oz carrots, sliced
250g/8oz tomatoes, skinned and sliced
1 teaspoon green mango powder
1 green chilli, chopped
15g/½oz root ginger, grated
1 teaspoon garam masala
1 tablespoon chopped coriander leaves
2 tablespoons melted butter

1 Melt the ghee in a large saucepan and fry the onion and garlic with the cumin for about 5 minutes until golden brown. Add the turmeric and shake the pan for a few seconds.

3 Add the tomatoes, green mango powder, chilli and ginger. Stir well and then replace the lid and continue cooking for 10 more minutes.

2 Add the cabbage, potatoes, peas and carrots. Cook, stirring continuously, for 5 minutes. Cover the pan and continue to cook gently over low heat for a further 10 minutes.

4 Add the garam masala and chopped coriander to the saucepan and stir well. Heat through over low heat for about 5 minutes. Serve hot with the melted butter poured over the top.

PREPARATION: 20 MINUTES
COOKING: 35 MINUTES
SERVES: 4-6

CAULIFLOWER CURRY

Gobi kari

125g/4oz ghee
pinch of asafoetida powder
750g/1½lb cauliflower, cut into florets
300ml/½ pint natural yogurt
2 large onions, finely chopped
2 garlic cloves, crushed
salt
4 bay leaves
300ml/½ pint hot water
For the spices:
6 cloves
6 black peppercorns
1 black cardamom
2 green cardamoms
2 x 2.5cm/1 inch pieces cinnamon stick
1 teaspoon coriander seeds
1 teaspoon white cumin seeds
1 teaspoon red chilli powder

1 Heat 25g/1oz of the ghee in a large saucepan with the asafoetida. Add the cauliflower and cook over medium heat for 5 minutes. Using a slotted spoon, transfer the cauliflower to a bowl and pour the yogurt over the top.

3 Return the cauliflower and yogurt to the pan and stir gently to combine all the ingredients. Cook gently over low heat for 10 minutes.

2 Add the remaining ghee to the pan and, when it is hot, add the onions, garlic, salt to taste, bay leaves and all the spices except the chilli powder. Fry until the onions are golden and soft, and then stir in the chilli powder.

4 Add the hot water and simmer, stirring occasionally, for 25 minutes, or until the cauliflower is tender. Serve this curry hot.

PREPARATION: 15 MINUTES
COOKING: 45 MINUTES
SERVES: 4-6

SPINACH WITH TOMATOES

Saag tamatar

1kg/2lb fresh spinach

175g/6oz ghee

2 large onions, thinly sliced

2 garlic cloves, thinly sliced

150g/5oz fresh root ginger

2 teaspoons chilli powder

2 teaspoons turmeric

2 teaspoons garam masala

2 teaspoons coriander seeds

1 teaspoon ground coriander

1 teaspoon cumin seeds

1½ teaspoons salt

2 teaspoons freshly ground black pepper

1 x 400g/13oz can tomatoes

2 Melt the ghee in a large, heavy-based saucepan and add the onions and garlic. Fry gently over moderate heat for about 5 minutes until they are golden and soft.

3 Meanwhile, peel the ginger and cut it into strips, about 3mm/⅛ inch thick. Add to the pan and cook gently for 5-6 minutes. Stir in the chilli powder, turmeric, garam masala, coriander seeds, ground coriander, cumin, salt and pepper, and cook for 1 minute.

4 Add the spinach and toss well to coat in the spice mixture. Add the tomatoes with their juice and bring to the boil, stirring. Add enough boiling water to prevent the spinach sticking to the bottom of the pan. Simmer for 5-10 minutes, until the spinach and tomatoes are cooked.

1 Wash the spinach thoroughly and then shake it dry. Remove any thick stalks and cut the spinach leaves into strips, about 2.5cm/1 inch wide.

PREPARATION: 15 MINUTES
COOKING: 20-25 MINUTES
SERVES: 4-6

BANANA CURRY

Kela kari

50g/2oz ghee
7.5cm/3 inch piece root ginger, peeled and thinly sliced
1 tablespoon garam masala
2 teaspoons cumin seeds
1 teaspoon chilli powder
1 teaspoon turmeric
1 teaspoon salt
1 teaspoon freshly ground black pepper
750g/1½lb under-ripe bananas
500ml/17 fl oz natural yogurt
juice of 1 lemon
fresh coriander leaves or parsley, to garnish

1 Melt the ghee in a large, heavy-based saucepan and gently fry the ginger for 4-5 minutes until soft. Add all the spices and stir well to mix with the ginger. Fry for a further 2 minutes.

3 Add the pieces of banana to the saucepan and turn them gently in the spice mixture until they are well coated all over.

2 Peel the bananas and then cut them into pieces about 2.5cm/1 inch long.

4 Mix the yogurt and lemon juice together in a bowl, and then pour slowly into the pan, stirring. Heat to just below boiling point, stirring constantly. Reduce the heat and simmer gently for 10 minutes, until the bananas are soft but not broken. Serve garnished with coriander or parsley.

PREPARATION: 5 MINUTES
COOKING: 25 MINUTES
SERVES: 6-8

STUFFED AUBERGINES

Baigan

1 Put the aubergines in a roasting pan with their cut sides upwards. Pour in the water, add the bay leaf and cover the pan tightly with foil. Poach in a preheated oven at 160°C/325°F/Gas Mark 3 for 25 minutes, or until soft.

2 Melt the ghee in a heavy-based saucepan and gently fry the onion and garlic for 4–5 minutes until soft. Crush the coriander seeds coarsely and add to the onion mixture with the chilli powder, lovage seeds and salt. Stir well and fry for 2–3 minutes.

3 Remove the poached aubergines from the water and pat dry with absorbent kitchen paper. With a teaspoon, scrape out the flesh, reserving the skins. Mash the flesh and add to the spice mixture. Fry for 2–3 minutes, stirring.

4-6 aubergines, halved lengthways
100ml/3½ fl oz water
1 bay leaf
125g/4oz ghee
1 large onion, finely chopped
2 garlic cloves, finely chopped
2 teaspoons coriander seeds
1 teaspoon chilli powder
1 teaspoon lovage seeds (optional)
1 teaspoon salt
To garnish:
fresh coriander leaves
dried red chillies, chopped

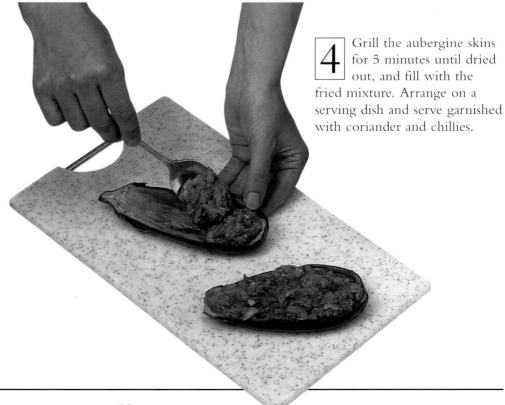

4 Grill the aubergine skins for 5 minutes until dried out, and fill with the fried mixture. Arrange on a serving dish and serve garnished with coriander and chillies.

PREPARATION: 20 MINUTES
COOKING: ABOUT 40 MINUTES
SERVES: 4-6

CREAM CHEESE KOFTA CURRY

Panir kofta kari

2 Mix the paneer with the coconut and remaining garam masala. Divide into 12 equal portions. Flatten the potato portions and use to wrap around the paneer portions. Roll into balls, brush with beaten egg white and fry in the ghee until golden brown. Drain and transfer to an ovenproof dish.

1 Boil the potatoes in some water with the green chilli, ginger and all but a pinch of the garam masala. When tender, drain the potatoes and mash with the salt, gram flour, breadcrumbs and coriander. Divide into 12 equal portions.

1kg/2lb potatoes, quartered
1 large fresh green chilli, chopped
1 teaspoon peeled and grated root ginger
1/2 teaspoon garam masala
salt
2 tablespoons gram flour
2 tablespoons fresh breadcrumbs
1 tablespoon roasted coriander seeds, ground
250g/8oz paneer (see page 111)
1 tablespoon grated or desiccated coconut
1 egg white, beaten
175g/6oz ghee
2 bay leaves
2 onions, chopped
6 garlic cloves, crushed
4 cloves
6 black peppercorns
150ml/1/4 pint natural yogurt
1 teaspoon turmeric
1 teaspoon chilli powder
500g/1lb tomatoes, skinned and sliced
2 tablespoons chopped coriander leaves

3 Add the bay leaves, onions, garlic, cloves and peppercorns to the ghee left in the pan, and fry until golden. Stir in the yogurt, turmeric and chilli powder. Add 300ml/1/2 pint water and bring to the boil. Simmer for 10 minutes.

4 Pour this sauce over the koftas and cover with the tomatoes and coriander leaves. Cook in a preheated oven at 180°C/350°F/Gas Mark 4 for 10-15 minutes, or until heated through. Serve immediately.

PREPARATION: 30 MINUTES
COOKING: ABOUT 1 HOUR
SERVES: 4-6

VEGETABLE ROLLS

Alu pura

5 medium potatoes, boiled and coarsely mashed

2 tablespoons chopped fresh coriander leaves

2 fresh green chillies, seeded and chopped

2 teaspoons lime juice

1 teaspoon garam masala

salt and freshly ground black pepper

oil for deep-frying

For the batters:

50g/2oz gram flour

175g/6oz plain flour

300ml/½ pint water

pinch of salt and chilli powder

1 teaspoon baking powder

300ml/½ pint milk

ghee for frying

To serve:

quick chutney (see page 111)

1 small onion, chopped

1 carrot, grated

¼ crisp lettuce, shredded

1 Make the filling for the pancake rolls: mix together the potatoes, coriander, chillies, lime juice, garam masala, salt and pepper. Shape the mixture into rolls, about 2.5cm/1 inch in diameter and 10cm/4 inches in length. Set aside.

3 Melt a little ghee in a small frying pan and pour in some pancake batter, swirling it around the pan to form a thick pancake. Cook until browned underneath and then flip over and cook the other side. Repeat with the remaining batter. Layer the pancakes with kitchen paper and keep warm.

2 Make the two batters: mix the gram flour with 50g/2oz of the plain flour and beat in the water to make a batter for the potato rolls. Add the salt and chilli powder and set aside. Mix the remaining plain flour with the baking powder and a pinch of salt. Beat in the milk to make a smooth pancake batter.

PREPARATION:
30 MINUTES
COOKING: 10–15 MINUTES
SERVES: 6

4 Heat the oil for deep-frying to 180°C/350°F. Dip the potato rolls in the prepared water batter and then deep-fry, a few at a time, until golden. Remove and drain. Spread each pancake with a little chutney and then top with a potato roll and some onion, carrot and lettuce. Fold over and serve.

SPICY OKRA

Bhindi bhaji

1 Peel one of the onions and then slice it very thinly. Heat the ghee in a heavy-based saucepan and add the sliced onion. Fry gently until tender and golden brown.

2 Peel and chop the remaining onion and garlic and place in a blender or food processor with the seasoning, coriander and turmeric. Process until the mixture is well blended.

3 Add the blended onion and spice mixture to the fried onions in the saucepan and cook over medium heat for 5 minutes, stirring occasionally.

| 2 large onions |
| 125g/4oz ghee |
| 4 garlic cloves |
| salt and freshly ground black pepper |
| 2 teaspoons ground coriander |
| ½ teaspoon turmeric |
| 500g/1lb fresh okra |
| 2 tomatoes, skinned and chopped |
| 1 teaspoon chopped fresh mint |
| ½ teaspoon garam masala |
| fresh mint to garnish |

4 Wash and dry the okra, and top and tail each one. Cut into 1cm/½ inch slices and add to the saucepan. Stir gently and then simmer, covered, for 20 minutes. Add the tomatoes, chopped mint and garam masala and simmer for 15 minutes. Serve garnished with fresh mint.

PREPARATION: 10 MINUTES
COOKING: 45 MINUTES
SERVES: 4

BATTER COILS IN SYRUP

Jalebi

1 Put the plain and gram flours in a large bowl and mix in the yogurt, yeast and water to make a thick creamy batter. Set aside for about 2 hours to ferment.

2 Put the water and sugar in a saucepan and stir over low heat until all the sugar has dissolved. Bring to the boil, still stirring, and cook until the syrup has reached the thread stage (107°C/225°F). Just before the syrup is ready, add the saffron powder and ground cardamom seeds.

3 Heat the vegetable oil until a cube of day-old bread turns golden in 1 minute. Whisk the batter thoroughly and then pour in a steady stream through a thin funnel or piping bag to form coils in the pan below. Make a few coils at a time, and deep-fry for about 30 seconds, turning them so that they are golden and crisp all over.

4 Remove the coils from the pan and drain on absorbent kitchen paper. Immerse them in the prepared syrup for 3-4 minutes to soak up as much syrup as possible. Remove and serve immediately while they are hot and crisp.

175g/6oz plain flour
50g/2oz gram flour, lightly dry-fried
4 tablespoons natural yogurt
5g/1/4 oz fresh yeast
300ml/1/2 pint water
250g/8oz sugar
1/2 teaspoon saffron powder
1/2 teaspoon green cardamom seeds, ground
vegetable oil for deep-frying

PREPARATION: 15 MINUTES +
STANDING TIME
COOKING: 15 MINUTES
SERVES: 4-6

COCONUT PUDDING

Beveca

1 Make some holes in the eyes of the coconuts and then carefully drain out the liquid over a bowl and reserve.

3 Gather up the muslin and squeeze out as much coconut milk as possible. Discard the coconut in the cloth. Mix the strained coconut milk with the liquid extracted from the coconuts, and then beat in all the remaining ingredients.

4 Pour the mixture into a large, heavy-based saucepan and bring to the boil. Reduce the heat and simmer until the liquid thickens, stirring constantly. Pour into a greased 20cm/ 8 inch round baking tin and bake in a preheated oven at 180°C/350°F/Gas Mark 4 for 30 minutes, until browned. Serve hot, garnished with coconut.

2 Crack open the coconuts and separate the flesh from the shells. Grate the flesh into a bowl and then pour over the boiling water. Leave to stand for 15 minutes, then strain the liquid through a sieve lined with double muslin, held over a bowl.

| 2 fresh coconuts |
| 450ml/³/₄ pint boiling water |
| 250g/8oz caster sugar |
| 175g/6oz rice flour |
| 2 eggs, beaten |
| 50g/2oz slivered almonds |
| shredded coconut, to decorate |

PREPARATION: 35 MINUTES
+ STANDING TIME
COOKING: 30 MINUTES
SERVES: 4

MANGO ICE CREAM

Am ka kulfi

1 Warm the mango pulp in a saucepan over gentle heat and then stir in the honey until melted. Remove from the heat and stir in the cream and the almonds until they are evenly mixed. Set aside until cool.

2 Pour the mango ice cream mixture into a freezer container and place in the freezer. Freeze for about 4 hours, or until the mango mixture is just beginning to freeze around the edges and to become slushy.

3 Remove the container from the freezer and turn out the mango ice cream into a bowl. Carefully break the mixture up with a fork.

425g/14oz canned mango pulp
3 tablespoons clear honey
600ml/1 pint double cream
50g/2oz ground almonds
4 egg whites
mint leaves, to decorate

4 Whisk the egg whites in a clean bowl until stiff, and then fold them gently into the half-frozen mixture. Return to the freezer container and freeze for a further 4 hours, or until solid. Remove the mixture from the freezer 20 minutes before serving to soften slightly. Decorate with mint leaves.

PREPARATION: 20 MINUTES
FREEZING: 8 HOURS
SERVES: 8

DEEP-FRIED MILK PASTRIES

Gulab jamun

1 Heat the milk in a saucepan, add the lemon juice and bring to the boil. Don't worry when the milk curdles. Boil for 5-10 minutes and then leave to cool. Drain off the whey, leaving the curds behind. Tie the curds up in a double thickness of muslin and place in a sieve. Weight down and leave overnight.

2 The following day, mix the resulting cheese (paneer) with the semolina to form a dough. Break into about 15 pieces and roll into smooth balls. Heat the oil for deep-frying until a ball of dough immediately starts to sizzle and floats to the surface when dropped into the pan.

| 1litre/1³/4 pints milk |
| juice of 2 lemons |
| 125g/4oz semolina |
| vegetable oil for deep-frying |
| **For the syrup:** |
| 300ml/¹/2 pint water |
| 5 cardamoms |
| 5 cloves |
| 250g/8oz sugar |
| 2 teaspoons rose water |

3 Deep-fry the balls, in batches, until evenly golden brown. Remove with a slotted spoon and drain on absorbent kitchen paper. Keep them warm in a low oven while you make the syrup.

4 Bring the water to the boil with the cardamoms and cloves. Reduce the heat, add the sugar and stir until dissolved. Increase the heat and boil rapidly, without stirring, until the syrup starts to thicken. Cool slightly and add the rose water. Serve the pastry balls warm in the syrup.

PREPARATION: 30 MINUTES
+ STANDING OVERNIGHT
COOKING: 25 MINUTES
SERVES: 4-6

BREAD STUFFED WITH DHAL
Puri

175g/6oz dried black beans
500g/1lb plain flour
1 fresh green chilli, chopped
½ teaspoon salt
vegetable oil for deep-frying
For the spices:
1 tablespoon aniseed
1 teaspoon coriander seeds
½ teaspoon white cumin seeds
½ teaspoon red chilli powder
¼ teaspoon asafoetida powder
coriander, to garnish

2 Grind the drained beans with the chilli, salt and all the spices to make the stuffing. You can do this in an electric grinder or food processor if wished. Mix well and divide into 16 portions.

3 With wet hands, divide the dough into 16 portions and smear each one with a little of the oil. Flatten each piece of dough and roll out to a 5cm/2 inch diameter round.

4 Wrap one portion of the stuffing in each round and, with greased hands, roll into smooth balls. Flatten each ball with a rolling pin into a 7.5cm/3 inch round. Heat the oil for deep-frying and fry the puri, one at a time, until golden on both sides. Drain on absorbent kitchen paper and serve garnished with coriander.

1 Soak the black beans in water overnight. Rinse them in clear water and drain well. Sift the flour into a bowl and gradually add enough cold water to make a soft dough. Cover with a damp cloth and then set aside for 30 minutes.

PREPARATION: 30 MINUTES
+ SOAKING AND STANDING
COOKING: 20 MINUTES
MAKES: 16

UNLEAVENED BREAD
Chapatis

1 Place the flour and salt in a bowl and make a well in the centre. Gradually stir in the water, a little at a time, and mix to a soft, supple dough.

2 Knead the dough on a lightly floured surface for 10 minutes, and then cover the dough and leave in a cool place for 30 minutes. Knead again very thoroughly and then divide the dough into 12 pieces.

3 Using a rolling pin, roll out each piece of dough into a thin round pancake on a lightly floured surface.

4 Lightly grease a griddle or heavy-based frying pan with a little ghee or oil and place over a moderate heat. Add a chapati to the pan and cook until blisters appear. Press down firmly with a fish slice and then turn it over and cook the other side until lightly coloured. Remove and keep warm while you cook the remaining chapatis. Serve brushed with a little butter and folded into quarters.

| 250g/8oz wholewheat flour |
| 1 teaspoon salt |
| 200ml/7 fl oz water |
| ghee or oil for greasing |
| butter for serving |

PREPARATION: 50 MINUTES
(INCLUDING STANDING TIME)
COOKING: 12 MINUTES
MAKES: 12

LEAVENED BREAD

Naan

1 Sift the flour into a large bowl and stir in the sugar, salt and baking powder. Dissolve the yeast in the milk and stir in the yogurt. Mix this well with the flour to form a dough.

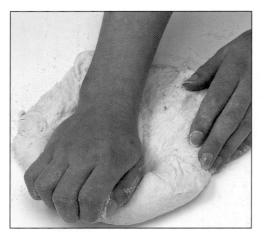

2 Knead the dough until it is smooth, and then place in a bowl covered with a clean cloth and leave it to rise in a warm place for about 4 hours.

PREPARATION: 30 MINUTES +
4 HOURS PROVING
COOKING: 30 MINUTES
MAKES: 12

3 Divide the risen dough into 12 equal portions and roll them into balls. On a lightly floured surface, flatten the balls into oblong shapes, using both hands and slapping the naan from one hand to the other.

375g/12oz plain flour
1½ teaspoons sugar
1 teaspoon salt
½ teaspoon baking powder
15g/½ oz fresh yeast
150ml/¼ pint warm milk
150ml/¼ pint natural yogurt
125g/4oz butter
2 tablespoons poppy seeds

4 Lightly grease a griddle or heavy-based frying pan and heat it until it is very hot. Cook the naan on one side only, a few at a time. Remove and spread the raw side with butter and poppy seeds. Cook under a preheated hot grill until browned. Serve hot.

SPICES, CHUTNEYS AND YOGURT

VINDALOO MASALA

15 cloves
4 cardamom pods, peeled
4 x 5cm/2 inch pieces cinnamon stick
4 bay leaves
8 dried red chillies
20 black peppercorns
1 tablespoon turmeric powder
1 tablespoon white cumin seeds
1 tablespoon black cumin seeds
4 tablespoons coriander seeds
1 1/2 teaspoons fenugreek seeds
1 1/2 teaspoons mustard seeds

Put all the spices in a heavy frying pan and roast over medium heat, stirring and shaking the pan constantly, for about 10 minutes, or until they release an aromatic smell. Take care that they do not burn. Grind to a fine powder in a mortar or electric grinder. Store in an airtight container for up to 3 months.

GARAM MASALA

15g/1/2oz black cumin seeds
15g/1/2oz white cumin seeds
75g/3oz coriander seeds
40g/1 1/2oz cardamom seeds
4 bay leaves
50g/2oz black peppercorns
15g/1/2oz grated nutmeg
15g/1/2oz blade mace
40g/1 1/2oz cinnamon sticks

Put all the ingredients in a heavy frying pan and roast over medium heat, stirring and shaking the pan to prevent the spices burning. Continue doing this for about 10 minutes, or until the spices darken and release their aroma. Place in a mortar or electric grinder and grind to a fine powder. Store in an airtight container for up to 3 months.

TANDOORI MASALA

1 teaspoon garlic powder
1 teaspoon ground ginger
1 teaspoon ground cloves
1 teaspoon ground mace
1/2 teaspoon grated nutmeg
2 tablespoons ground coriander
1 1/2 teaspoons ground cumin
1 teaspoon ground fenugreek seeds
1 teaspoon ground cinnamon
1 teaspoon ground black pepper
1 teaspoon ground cardamom seeds
2 teaspoons paprika
2 teaspoons red food colouring

Put all the ingredients in a bowl and mix well together. Push the mixture through a fine sieve and store in an airtight container. It will keep for up to 3 months.

SAMOSA DOUGH

500g/1lb plain flour
1 teaspoon salt
175g/6oz soft margarine
150ml/1/4 pint water

Sift the flour and salt into a large mixing bowl. Cut the margarine into small pieces and rub it into the flour with your fingertips, until the mixture resembles fine breadcrumbs. Stir in the water, a little at a time, until it is all amalgamated. Knead thoroughly until you have a smooth dough. Cover with a damp cloth and leave for about 15 minutes before rolling out and using to make samosas. This amount of dough is enough to make 12 samosas.

COCONUT CREAM AND MILK

300g/11oz desiccated coconut
750ml/1 1/4 pints boiling water

Put the desiccated coconut and boiling water in an electric blender and work for 20 seconds. Pour into a bowl and leave to cool to until it is tepid. Strain the mixture into a clean bowl or jug. This is the coconut milk. When the cream rises to the top of the milk, skim it off. This is the coconut cream.

YOGURT RAITA

150ml/5 fl oz natural yogurt
1/2 small cucumber, cut into small dice
2 spring onions, finely chopped
15-20 mint leaves, finely chopped
1/2 garlic clove, crushed
1 fresh green chilli, seeded and finely chopped
salt and freshly ground black pepper

Put the yogurt in a bowl and beat lightly. Stir in the cucumber, spring onions, mint, garlic and chilli. Season to taste with salt and pepper. Cover and leave to chill in the refrigerator for at least 1 hour. Serve with kebabs and curries and other Indian dishes. This amount serves 4-6.

QUICK CHUTNEY

1 large bunch of fresh coriander leaves
3 fresh green chillies, seeded and chopped
1 teaspoon sugar
1/2 teaspoon salt
3 tablespoons grated fresh coconut
juice of 1/2 lime

Trim the stalks from the coriander and grind the leaves with the chillies, sugar, salt, coconut and lime juice to form a paste. You can do this either by pounding in a mortar or by grinding in an electric blender. Serve with savoury dishes. This is enough to serve 4-6 people.

PANEER
Indian curd cheese

1 1/2 litres/2 pints creamy milk
juice of 1 lemon or 2 tablespoons vinegar or 4 tablespoons natural yogurt

Bring the milk to the boil in a heavy-based saucepan. Reduce the heat and add the lemon juice, vinegar or yogurt. Do not worry when the milk curdles.

Stir gently for about 1 minute, until the curds separate from the whey. It is important to stir extremely gently so that the curds stay in large pieces and don't break up in to smaller ones. Remove from the heat.

Line a large sieve or colander with several thicknesses of muslin and pour in the curd mixture. Hold under a gently running cold tap for a few seconds. Gather up the 4 corners of the muslin and tie together. Now twist gently to extract as much moisture as possible, then hang the bag up and leave the cheese to drain for 1 1/2 hours, until crumbly. Place the cheese, still in the muslin bag, on a work surface and shape into a block. Cover with a board and leave, weighted down, for 2 hours. Cut into squares and use in sweet and savoury dishes.

GHEE

450g/1lb unsalted butter

Cut the butter into small dice and place in a heavy-based saucepan. Melt slowly over very low heat, about 5-15 minutes. Raise the heat to moderate, and when a thin layer of white foam appears on the surface, simmer without stirring until the foam subsides, about 10 minutes.

Stir constantly until the solids at the base of the pan turn brown. Remove from the heat and skim the scum off the surface. Leave to cool and then strain through a double thickness of muslin into a screwtop jar. Store the ghee in the refrigerator and use as required.

BIRIYANI SPICES

4 cloves
8 black peppercorns
4 green cardamoms
1 black cardamom, crushed
1 x 5cm/2 inch cinnamon stick
1/2 teaspoon turmeric

Mix the spices together without grinding and use fresh to flavour chicken or duck biriyani. This mixture is sufficient for a biriyani to serve 4 people.

BOMBAY MIXTURE

4-5 small dried chillies
1 x 5cm/2 inch cinnamon stick
4 1/2 tablespoons coriander seeds
1 teaspoon cumin seeds
1/2 teaspoon fennel seeds
1/2 teaspoon fenugreek seeds
1/2 teaspoon garlic powder
2 1/2 teaspoons turmeric
2 kokum skins (optional)
2 crushed curry leaves

Lightly roast the chillies, cinnamon stick, coriander, cumin, fennel and fenugreek seeds. Grind them in a mortar or electric grinder and mix with the garlic powder and turmeric. When adding to a curry, stir into the pot with the kokum skins and curry leaves.

INDIAN YOGURT

600ml/1 pint creamy milk
2 tablespoons natural yogurt

Put the milk in a heavy-based saucepan and bring to the boil, stirring all the time to prevent a skin forming. Remove from the heat and set aside for about 10 minutes until the milk has cooled to 55°C/130°F. Remove any skin from the surface.

Beat the yogurt and stir into the milk. Pour into a bowl and cover with a clean tea-towel. Leave overnight in a warm place until thickened. Transfer the yogurt to a sealed container and store in the refrigerator.

INDEX